Uthmani

NASKH VERSION

HANDWRITTEN TRACEABLE METHOD

JUZ AMMA TRACE

INTERNATIONAL EDITION
AUTHENTIC MEDINA SCRIPT

International Version
First Edition

JUZ BY JUZ SERIES

**JUZ AMMA TRACE
JUZ TABARAK TRACE
JUZ QAD SAMI TRACE**

Medina Uthmani Script
Naskh Font Calligraphy
Fifteen Lined Format
Hafs (Aasim) Variant

Quran Copy of Medina Saudi Arabia
Designed in the United Kingdom
Published by Fayrouz Media
Printed in Istanbul Turkey

*A copy of this book has been deposited with
the Legal Deposit Office of the British Library*

Distribution & Wholesale

info@qurantrace.com
www.qurantrace.com

Juz Amma ISBN: 978-1-7394115-1-0
Juz Tabarak ISBN: 978-1-7394115-4-1
Juz Qad Sami ISBN: 978-1-7394115-5-8

*This edition of the Holy Quran has received official
verification from the El Badr Quran Institute, and is globally
recognized and accredited by esteemed Quranic scholars*

**All Rights Reserved
Copyright © 2024**

SURAH AL-ALAQ

Read, and your Lord is the most gracious,
who imparted knowledge by means of the pen.
He taught man what he did not know.

CONTENTS

SURAH	PAGE	سورة
Al-Fatihah		الفاتحة
An-Naba'	1	النبأ
An-Naazi'aat	2	النازعات
Abasa	4	عبس
At-Takweer	5	التكوير
Al-Infitar	6	الإنفطار
Al-Mutaffifeen	6	المطففين
Al-Inshiqaaq	8	الانشقاق
Al-Burooj	9	البروج
At-Taariq	10	الطارق
Al-A'laa	10	الأعلى
Al-Ghaashiyah	11	الغاشية
Al-Fajr	12	الفجر
Al-Balad	13	البلد
Ash-Shams	14	الشمس
Al-Layl	14	الليل
Ad-Dhuha	15	الضحى
Ash-Sharh	15	الشرح
At-Tin	16	التين
Al-Alaq	16	العلق
Al-Qadr	17	القدر
Al-Bayyinah	17	البينة
Az-Zalzalah	18	الزلزلة
Al-'Aadiyat	18	العاديات
Al-Qaari'ah	19	القارعة
At-Takaathur	19	التكاثر
Al-'Asr	20	العصر
Al-Humazah	20	الهُمَزَة
Al-Feel	20	الفيل
Quraish	21	قريش
Al-Maa'oon	21	الماعون
Al-Kawthar	21	الكوثر
Al-Kaafiroon	22	الكافرون
An-Nasr	22	النصر
Al-Masad	22	المسد
Al-Ikhlas	23	الإخلاص
Al-Falaq	23	الفلق
An-Naas	23	الناس

WRITING GUIDELINES

It is necessary to keep in mind that when we write the Quran, we are actually writing the words of Allah, the Almighty. As a result, we'll adhere to a mannered approach that is respectful and keeps the traditional approach in mind. In order to follow the Arabic text, we shall use the handwritten traceable approach. According to the Arabic text of the Quran, the correct writing orientation is from top right to bottom left; writing in the contrary manner is not advised.

Following are the recommended procedures for writing/tracing the Quran according to the relevant rules with additional points to consider noted at the bottom:

■ It is obligatory to complete the wudhu ritual of washing in Islam before writing.
■ Use a quality pen or pencil, make sure the ink does not transfer to the next page.
■ Writing must be done in a specific order, i.e. by beginning from the first word of the verse. It's not a recommended practice to write randomly or in reverse order.
■ Maintain a high level of focus whilst writing, to avoid mistakes. Using a pencil with an eraser is recommended for the beginner which will give an option to re-trace.
■ Locate a suitable, comfortable writing location, such as a firm, flat surface.
■ Make an effort to finish page by page or Surah by Surah.

■■■■ STEP ONE - *Rasm*

Writing a group of key letters. The first thing that needs to be finished are the main body of the letters. This might be a complete word or a full phrase. The Rasm is the oldest part of the Arabic script; it has 18 elements, excluding the ligature of lām and alif. When isolated and in the final position, the 18 letters are visually distinct.

۞ الْحَمْدُ لِلَّهِ رَبِّ الْعَلَمِينَ ﴿٢﴾

■■■■ STEP TWO - *I'jām*

Write the dots in the already-written letters when the body of letters is complete. The i'jām (sometimes also called nuqat) are the diacritic points that distinguish various consonants that have the same form, rasm.

۞ الْحَمْدُ لِلَّهِ رَبِّ الْعَلَمِينَ ﴿٢﴾

■■■■ STEP THREE - *Harakāt*

After finishing the dots and writing the letter bodies, Harakāt can be written. Harakāt which literally means 'motions', are the short vowel marks. There is some ambiguity as to which tashkīl are also Harakāt; the tanwīn, for example, are markers for both vowels and consonants.

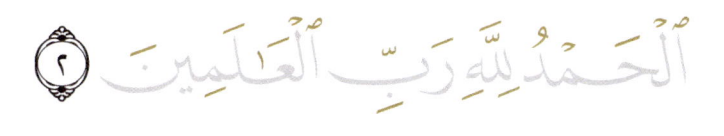

10 ETIQUETTES

INSPIRED BY IMAM AL QURTUBI RH

Key observation points:

1. The Holy Qur'an should be treated with respect and reverence. It should not be placed on the floor or handled carelessly. They are the words of Allah and should be given highest importance.

2. When holding the Holy Qur'an, it is recommended to have clean hands and to avoid touching the text with dirty or impure hands. It is obligatory to perform ablutions (wudhu) before handling the Qur'an, as a sign of respect and purity.

3. The Holy Qur'an should be kept in a clean, safe place and should not be placed next to any impure or unclean objects. The Qur'an should not be used as a prop or for any other purpose other than reading and studying its teachings.

4. It is recommended to recite du'a (supplications) before handling the Holy Qur'an and to take refuge in Allah from the accursed Devil with isti'aatha and to say the Basmala.

5. When reading from the Holy Qur'an, it is highly recommended to recite with proper pronunciation and to recite with respect and reverence. To give each letter its due so as to clearly and fully pronounce every word, for each letter counts as ten good deeds.

6. When not in prayer, to sit up straight, to avoid slouching, to face the direction of prayer (qiblah), and to close the Qur'an if it is put down. Not to rest on the Qur'an or use it as a pillow, and not to throw it away when passing it to someone else.

7. Even if one is not Muslim, treating the Qur'an with respect is advised. Before handling the Qur'an, non-Muslims should obtain permission and treat it with reverence. Placing the Qur'an in a location where it can be walked on or sat on is disrespectful.

8. To pause at verses that promise Allah's favour, to long for Allah Most High and ask of His bounty; and at verses that warn of His punishment to ask Him to save one from it.

9. To read the Qur'an every day, at least once, and to start over if one has finished reciting it completely so that it doesn't appear to be something that has been left behind.

10. Using one's intellect and knowledge to understand what is being spoken to one as well as learning the meanings of the Qur'anic lexical usages.

GEMS DERIVED FROM AL-JAMI' LI AHKAM AL-QUR'AN

BENEFITS

Master your Arabic reading, writing and pronunciation

Tracing offers a unique and effective way to enhance your language skills, empowering you to grasp the intricacies of the written form, improve your handwriting, enhance your visual recognition, and refine your speaking abilities.

Allowing you to observe the intricate strokes and shapes of each letter, tracing the words of the Quran will give you the unique opportunity to immerse yourself in the visual representation of the Arabic language and familiarize yourself with the specific nuances of the Quran's script. Whether it's the elegant curves of the individual letters or the intricate characters of the vowel system, Quran Trace will strengthen your visual recognition and reading abilities.

By repeatedly tracing the letters, you'll also train your muscles to recreate the shapes accurately, resulting in clearer and more legible handwriting. This will aid in reinforcing the connections between reading and writing, allowing for a more comprehensive language learning experience. As you trace the curves, lines and dots of the Arabic script, you'll become intimately acquainted with the rhythm and flow of the language, cultivating a natural sense of its tempo and intonation. This acquired sense of rhythm is invaluable when it comes to speaking and reciting, enabling you to develop a more authentic and native-like accent.

Accelerate your Arabic comprehension

Writing is a highly effective tool for consolidating your grasp of grammar and vocabulary. By tracing the Quran, you'll reinforce your understanding of Arabic sentence structure, verb conjugation, and word usage. Writing out each and every predetermined verse will allow you to internalize Arabic language patterns and expand your linguistic repertoire with ultimate accuracy, enhancing your ability to experience the precision and eloquence of Allah's words.

Tracing is an active engagement that enables you to internalise the language on a deeper level. So, whether you're a novice learner or an experienced polyglot, make Quran Trace an integral part of your language acquisition toolkit. Embrace the transformative power it offers and witness your language skills flourish! accent.

Consolidate your memorisation

Quran Trace invites you to partake in the deeply rooted practice of writing for memorisation found in many parts of Africa, including Mauritania, Sudan and Morocco. In this region, it's customary for students of the Quran to repetitively write verses on a lawh (wooden board) until they are accurately committed to memory.

Scientific research has also consistently shown that writing is an exceptional tool for improving memorization. The act of writing stimulates multiple regions of the brain, including those responsible for language processing, cognition, and memory recall. By actively participating in the process, you create a unique connection between the information you're writing and your own neural pathways.

BENEFITS

Revive the Islamic tradition of penmanship

Islamic penmanship holds a significant place in Islamic art and culture. Islamic calligraphy is the artistic practice of writing the Arabic script in a highly decorative and stylized manner. It is considered a major form of artistic expression within Islamic cultures, with a rich history that spans centuries.

The art of calligraphy developed as a means to beautifully transcribe and preserve the sacred text of the Quran, with skilled calligraphers who practice this art form being highly revered. Quran Trace offers you the opportunity to partake in this rich tradition of preservation by completing the handwriting of the Quran in the naskh calligraphy style.

For the complete novice or the experienced calligrapher, you've got the full Juz to brush up on your skills! The naskh font is a more rounded and fluid script style that emerged in the 10th century. It is highly readable and versatile, making it suitable for all ages and abilities.

Connect with Allah

The Quran is the rope of Allah, a guidance and gift for all humankind. Such an important lifeline deserves our utmost attention, and Quran Trace provides a quiet sanctuary for just this. Forced to slow down, tracing every letter of the Holy Book, it serves as a personal retreat where you'll have time to ponder Allah's words, contemplate, seek guidance, and delve into the depths of taddabur.

The act of reciting and memorising the Qura itself is highly regarded and carries numerous blessings and rewards, both in this world and in the hereafter. With every letter carrying its own reward, and that reward being multiplied by ten, imagine the reward for reading and writing each individual letter!

Cultivate positive, Quran-centred lifestyle habits

In our fast-paced, technology-driven world, finding moments of inner calm and clarity can be a challenge. However, through the simple act of writing, you can unlock a multitude of benefits for your mental well-being.

Quran Trace serves as a gateway to mindfulness, allowing you to fully immerse yourself in the present moment. The act of tracing works as a cognitive distraction, shifting your attention away from stressors and creating a sacred space where you can detach. As you put pen to paper, you'll become acutely aware of your thoughts, feelings, and surroundings. In this state of mindfulness, stress melts away, replaced by a sense of tranquillity and inner peace. It also enhances concentration by sharpening your focus and honing your attention to detail.

Through this process, your concentration muscles strengthen, and your ability to sustain focus in other areas of life may significantly improve. Tracing becomes a gateway to a heightened sense of awareness where you can fully immerse yourself in the task at hand.

*In the Name of Allah,
the Most Beneficent,
the Most Merciful.*

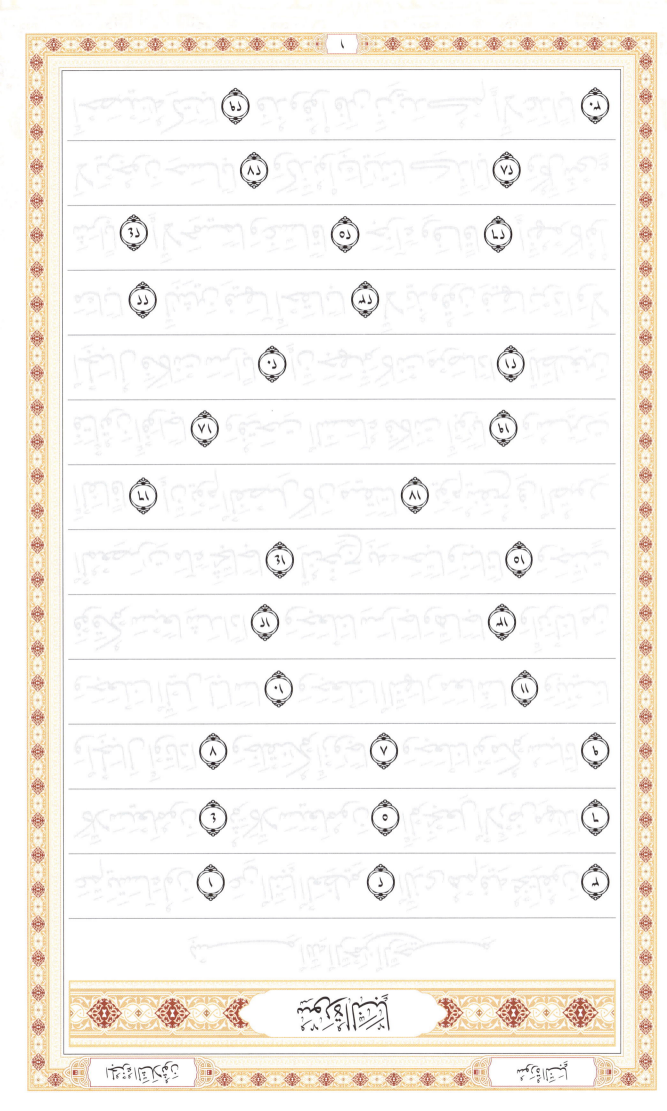

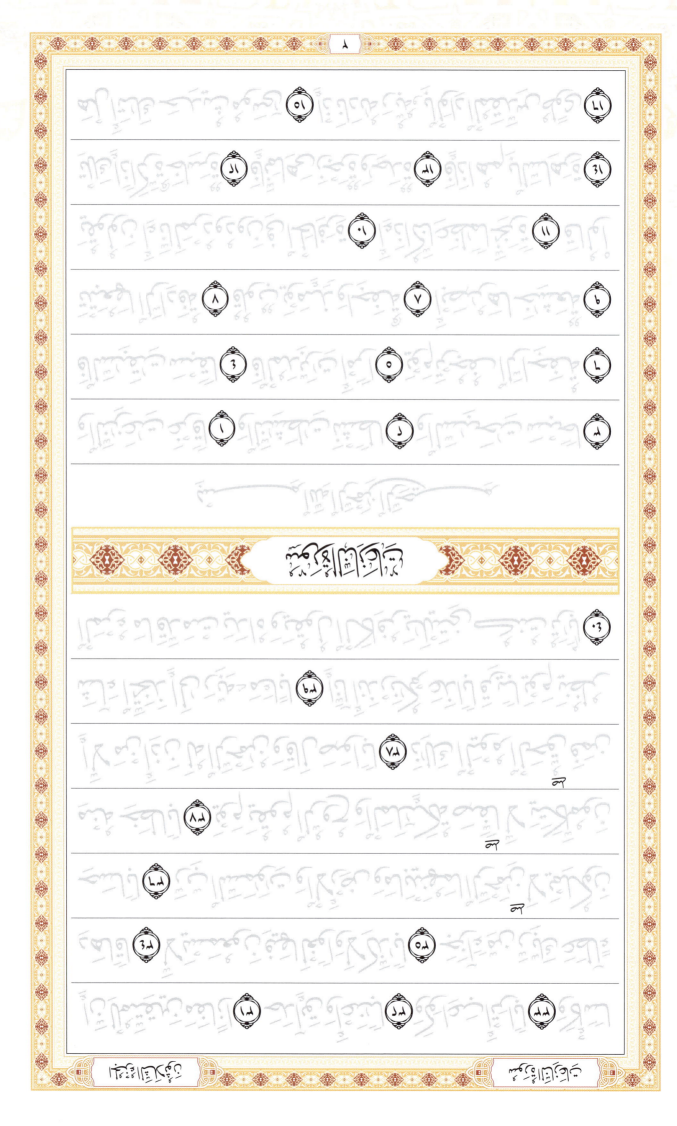

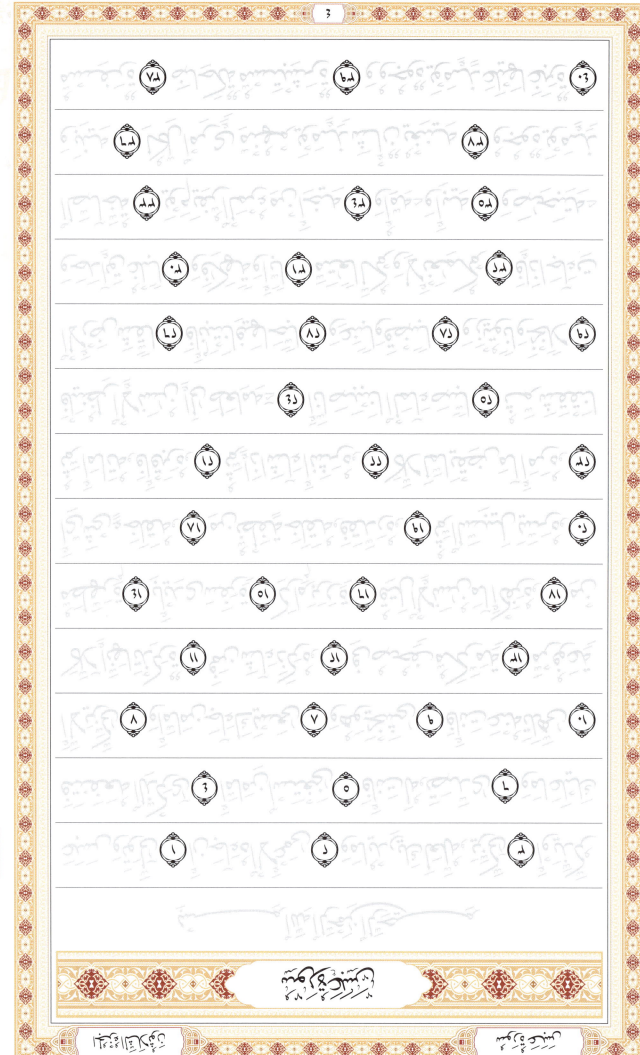

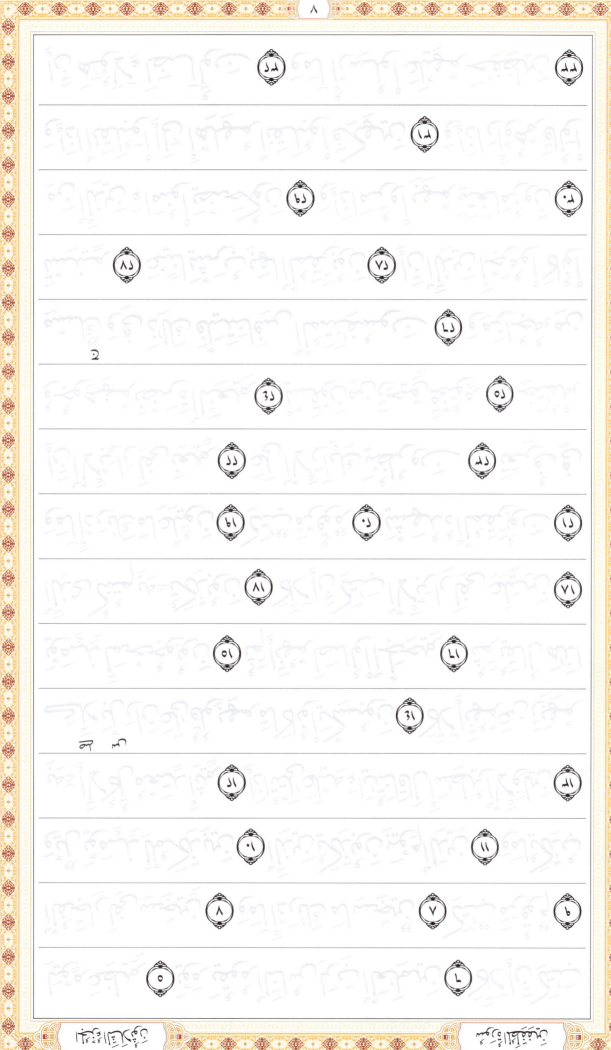

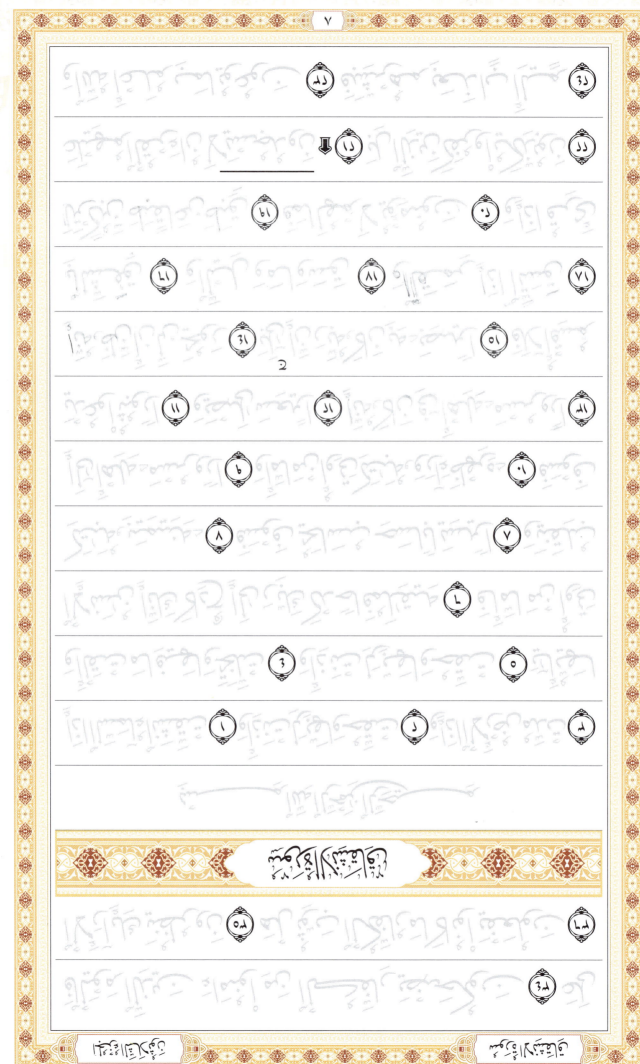

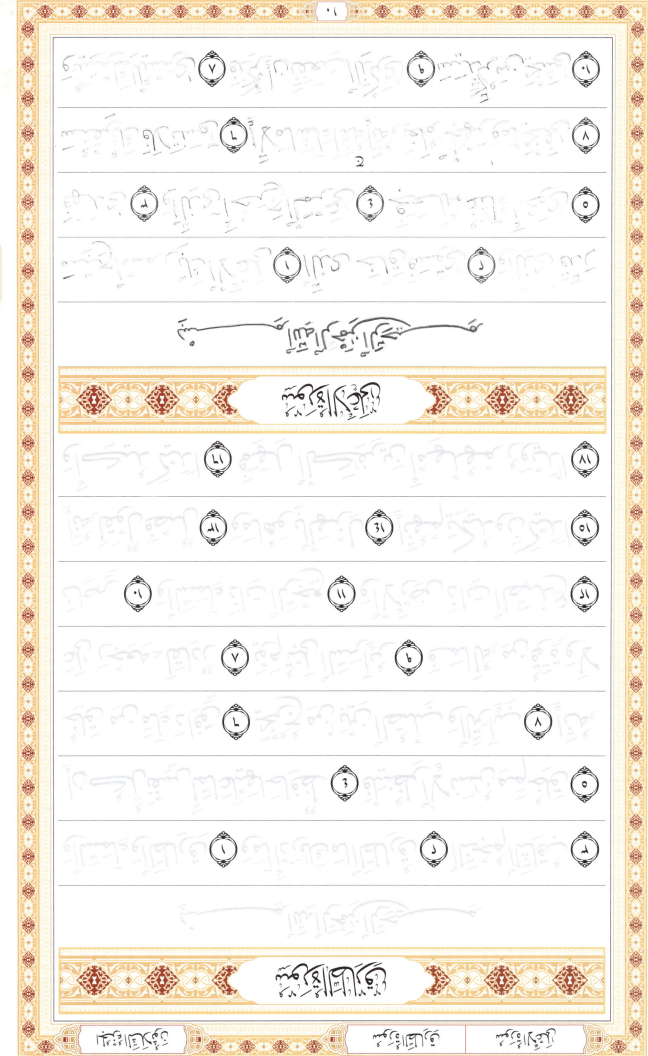

الجزء الثلاثون — سورة البلد

وَجَآءَ يَوْمَئِذٍ بِجَهَنَّمَ يَوْمَئِذٍ يَتَذَكَّرُ الْإِنسَانُ وَأَنَّىٰ

لَهُ الذِّكْرَىٰ ﴿٢٣﴾ يَقُولُ يَا لَيْتَنِي قَدَّمْتُ لِحَيَاتِي ﴿٢٤﴾ فَيَوْمَئِذٍ

لَّا يُعَذِّبُ عَذَابَهُ أَحَدٌ ﴿٢٦﴾ ﴿٢٥﴾ وَلَا يُوثِقُ وَثَاقَهُ أَحَدٌ يَا أَيَّتُهَا

النَّفْسُ الْمُطْمَئِنَّةُ ﴿٢٨﴾ ﴿٢٧﴾ ارْجِعِي إِلَىٰ رَبِّكِ رَاضِيَةً مَّرْضِيَّةً

فَادْخُلِي فِي عِبَادِي ﴿٣٠﴾ ﴿٢٩﴾ وَادْخُلِي جَنَّتِي

سورة البلد

بِسْمِ اللَّهِ الرَّحْمَٰنِ الرَّحِيمِ

لَا أُقْسِمُ بِهَٰذَا الْبَلَدِ ﴿٣﴾ ﴿٢﴾ وَأَنتَ حِلٌّ بِهَٰذَا الْبَلَدِ ﴿١﴾ وَوَالِدٍ وَمَا وَلَدَ

لَقَدْ خَلَقْنَا الْإِنسَانَ فِي كَبَدٍ ﴿٤﴾ أَيَحْسَبُ أَن لَّن يَقْدِرَ عَلَيْهِ

أَحَدٌ ﴿٧﴾ ﴿٦﴾ يَقُولُ أَهْلَكْتُ مَالًا لُّبَدًا ﴿٥﴾ أَيَحْسَبُ أَن لَّمْ يَرَهُ أَحَدٌ

أَلَمْ نَجْعَل لَّهُ عَيْنَيْنِ ﴿٨﴾ وَلِسَانًا وَشَفَتَيْنِ ﴿٩﴾ وَهَدَيْنَاهُ

النَّجْدَيْنِ ﴿١٢﴾ ﴿١١﴾ فَلَا اقْتَحَمَ الْعَقَبَةَ ﴿١٠﴾ وَمَا أَدْرَاكَ مَا الْعَقَبَةُ

فَكُّ رَقَبَةٍ ﴿١٣﴾ أَوْ إِطْعَامٌ فِي يَوْمٍ ذِي مَسْغَبَةٍ ﴿١٤﴾ يَتِيمًا ذَا مَقْرَبَةٍ ﴿١٥﴾

أَوْ مِسْكِينًا ذَا مَتْرَبَةٍ ﴿١٦﴾ ثُمَّ كَانَ مِنَ الَّذِينَ آمَنُوا وَتَوَاصَوْا

بِالصَّبْرِ وَتَوَاصَوْا بِالْمَرْحَمَةِ ﴿١٧﴾ أُولَٰئِكَ أَصْحَابُ الْمَيْمَنَةِ ﴿١٨﴾

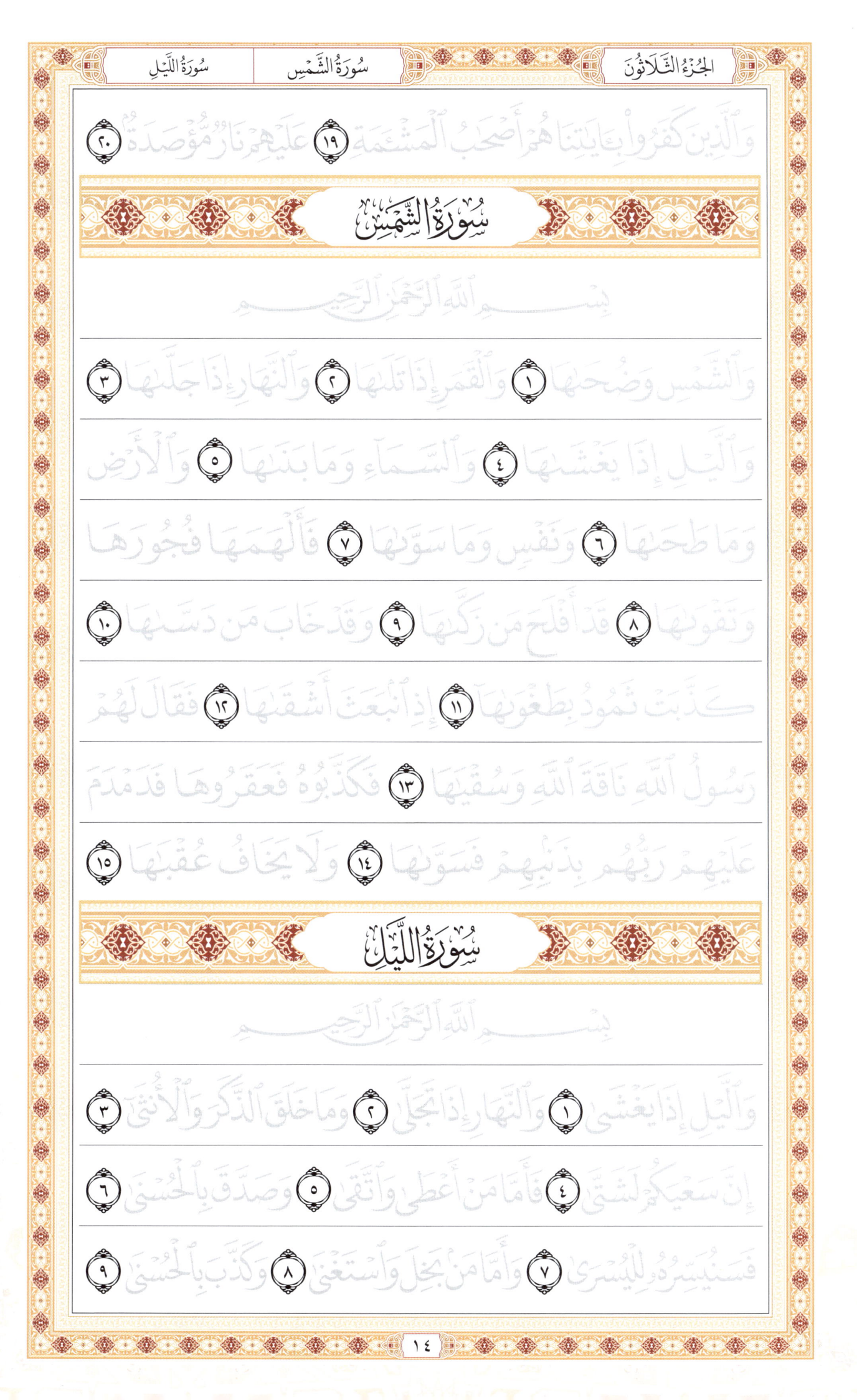

الجزء الثلاثون | سورة الشمس | سورة الليل

وَٱلَّذِينَ كَفَرُوا۟ بِـَٔايَٰتِنَا هُمْ أَصْحَٰبُ ٱلْمَشْـَٔمَةِ ﴿١٩﴾ عَلَيْهِمْ نَارٌ مُّؤْصَدَةٌۢ ﴿٢٠﴾

سُورَةُ الشَّمْسِ

بِسْمِ ٱللَّهِ ٱلرَّحْمَٰنِ ٱلرَّحِيمِ

وَٱلشَّمْسِ وَضُحَىٰهَا ﴿١﴾ وَٱلْقَمَرِ إِذَا تَلَىٰهَا ﴿٢﴾ وَٱلنَّهَارِ إِذَا جَلَّىٰهَا ﴿٣﴾

وَٱلَّيْلِ إِذَا يَغْشَىٰهَا ﴿٤﴾ وَٱلسَّمَآءِ وَمَا بَنَىٰهَا ﴿٥﴾ وَٱلْأَرْضِ

وَمَا طَحَىٰهَا ﴿٦﴾ وَنَفْسٍ وَمَا سَوَّىٰهَا ﴿٧﴾ فَأَلْهَمَهَا فُجُورَهَا

وَتَقْوَىٰهَا ﴿٨﴾ قَدْ أَفْلَحَ مَن زَكَّىٰهَا ﴿٩﴾ وَقَدْ خَابَ مَن دَسَّىٰهَا ﴿١٠﴾

كَذَّبَتْ ثَمُودُ بِطَغْوَىٰهَآ ﴿١١﴾ إِذِ ٱنۢبَعَثَ أَشْقَىٰهَا ﴿١٢﴾ فَقَالَ لَهُمْ

رَسُولُ ٱللَّهِ نَاقَةَ ٱللَّهِ وَسُقْيَٰهَا ﴿١٣﴾ فَكَذَّبُوهُ فَعَقَرُوهَا فَدَمْدَمَ

عَلَيْهِمْ رَبُّهُم بِذَنۢبِهِمْ فَسَوَّىٰهَا ﴿١٤﴾ وَلَا يَخَافُ عُقْبَٰهَا ﴿١٥﴾

سُورَةُ الليْلِ

بِسْمِ ٱللَّهِ ٱلرَّحْمَٰنِ ٱلرَّحِيمِ

وَٱلَّيْلِ إِذَا يَغْشَىٰ ﴿١﴾ وَٱلنَّهَارِ إِذَا تَجَلَّىٰ ﴿٢﴾ وَمَا خَلَقَ ٱلذَّكَرَ وَٱلْأُنثَىٰٓ ﴿٣﴾

إِنَّ سَعْيَكُمْ لَشَتَّىٰ ﴿٤﴾ فَأَمَّا مَنْ أَعْطَىٰ وَٱتَّقَىٰ ﴿٥﴾ وَصَدَّقَ بِٱلْحُسْنَىٰ ﴿٦﴾

فَسَنُيَسِّرُهُۥ لِلْيُسْرَىٰ ﴿٧﴾ وَأَمَّا مَنۢ بَخِلَ وَٱسْتَغْنَىٰ ﴿٨﴾ وَكَذَّبَ بِٱلْحُسْنَىٰ ﴿٩﴾

الجزء الثلاثون	سورة الضحى	سورة الشرح

فَسَنُيَسِّرُهُ لِلْعُسْرَىٰ ⑩ وَمَا يُغْنِي عَنْهُ مَالُهُ إِذَا تَرَدَّىٰ ⑪ إِنَّ عَلَيْنَا

لَلْهُدَىٰ ⑫ وَإِنَّ لَنَا لَلْآخِرَةَ وَالْأُولَىٰ ⑬ فَأَنذَرْتُكُمْ نَارًا تَلَظَّىٰ ⑭

لَا يَصْلَاهَا إِلَّا الْأَشْقَى ⑮ الَّذِي كَذَّبَ وَتَوَلَّىٰ ⑯ وَسَيُجَنَّبُهَا

الْأَتْقَى ⑰ الَّذِي يُؤْتِي مَالَهُ يَتَزَكَّىٰ ⑱ وَمَا لِأَحَدٍ عِندَهُ مِن نِّعْمَةٍ

تُجْزَىٰ ⑲ إِلَّا ابْتِغَاءَ وَجْهِ رَبِّهِ الْأَعْلَىٰ ⑳ وَلَسَوْفَ يَرْضَىٰ ㉑

سُورَةُ الضُّحَىٰ

بِسْمِ اللَّهِ الرَّحْمَٰنِ الرَّحِيمِ

وَالضُّحَىٰ ① وَاللَّيْلِ إِذَا سَجَىٰ ② مَا وَدَّعَكَ رَبُّكَ وَمَا قَلَىٰ ③

وَلَلْآخِرَةُ خَيْرٌ لَّكَ مِنَ الْأُولَىٰ ④ وَلَسَوْفَ يُعْطِيكَ رَبُّكَ

فَتَرْضَىٰ ⑤ أَلَمْ يَجِدْكَ يَتِيمًا فَآوَىٰ ⑥ وَوَجَدَكَ ضَالًّا فَهَدَىٰ ⑦

وَوَجَدَكَ عَائِلًا فَأَغْنَىٰ ⑧ فَأَمَّا الْيَتِيمَ فَلَا تَقْهَرْ ⑨

وَأَمَّا السَّائِلَ فَلَا تَنْهَرْ ⑩ وَأَمَّا بِنِعْمَةِ رَبِّكَ فَحَدِّثْ ⑪

سُورَةُ الشَّرْحِ

بِسْمِ اللَّهِ الرَّحْمَٰنِ الرَّحِيمِ

أَلَمْ نَشْرَحْ لَكَ صَدْرَكَ ① وَوَضَعْنَا عَنكَ وِزْرَكَ ②

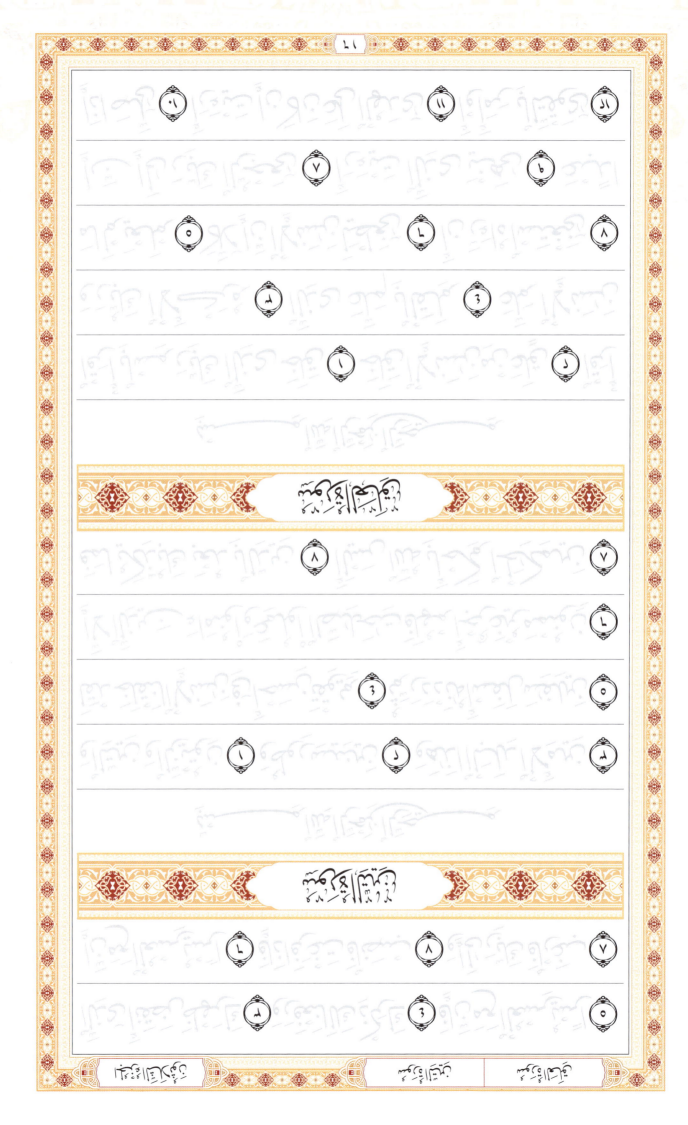

| الجزء الثلاثون | سورةُ القَدر | سورةُ البَيِّنَة |

سَجدَة

أَرَءَيْتَ إِن كَذَّبَ وَتَوَلَّىٰ ۝١٣ أَلَمْ يَعْلَم بِأَنَّ ٱللَّهَ يَرَىٰ ۝١٤ كَلَّا لَئِن لَّمْ يَنتَهِ

لَنَسْفَعًۢا بِٱلنَّاصِيَةِ ۝١٥ نَاصِيَةٍ كَٰذِبَةٍ خَاطِئَةٍ ۝١٦ فَلْيَدْعُ نَادِيَهُۥ ۝١٧

سَنَدْعُ ٱلزَّبَانِيَةَ ۝١٨ كَلَّا لَا تُطِعْهُ وَٱسْجُدْ وَٱقْتَرِب ۩ ۝١٩

سُورَةُ القَدر

بِسْمِ ٱللَّهِ ٱلرَّحْمَٰنِ ٱلرَّحِيمِ

إِنَّآ أَنزَلْنَٰهُ فِى لَيْلَةِ ٱلْقَدْرِ ۝١ وَمَآ أَدْرَىٰكَ مَا لَيْلَةُ ٱلْقَدْرِ ۝٢

لَيْلَةُ ٱلْقَدْرِ خَيْرٌ مِّنْ أَلْفِ شَهْرٍ ۝٣ تَنَزَّلُ ٱلْمَلَٰٓئِكَةُ وَٱلرُّوحُ فِيهَا

بِإِذْنِ رَبِّهِم مِّن كُلِّ أَمْرٍ ۝٤ سَلَٰمٌ هِىَ حَتَّىٰ مَطْلَعِ ٱلْفَجْرِ ۝٥

سُورَةُ البَيِّنَة

بِسْمِ ٱللَّهِ ٱلرَّحْمَٰنِ ٱلرَّحِيمِ

لَمْ يَكُنِ ٱلَّذِينَ كَفَرُوا۟ مِنْ أَهْلِ ٱلْكِتَٰبِ وَٱلْمُشْرِكِينَ مُنفَكِّينَ حَتَّىٰ

تَأْتِيَهُمُ ٱلْبَيِّنَةُ ۝١ رَسُولٌ مِّنَ ٱللَّهِ يَتْلُوا۟ صُحُفًا مُّطَهَّرَةً ۝٢ فِيهَا كُتُبٌ

قَيِّمَةٌ ۝٣ وَمَا تَفَرَّقَ ٱلَّذِينَ أُوتُوا۟ ٱلْكِتَٰبَ إِلَّا مِنۢ بَعْدِ مَا جَآءَتْهُمُ

ٱلْبَيِّنَةُ ۝٤ وَمَآ أُمِرُوٓا۟ إِلَّا لِيَعْبُدُوا۟ ٱللَّهَ مُخْلِصِينَ لَهُ ٱلدِّينَ

حُنَفَآءَ وَيُقِيمُوا۟ ٱلصَّلَوٰةَ وَيُؤْتُوا۟ ٱلزَّكَوٰةَ وَذَٰلِكَ دِينُ ٱلْقَيِّمَةِ ۝٥

الجزء الثلاثون   سورة الزلزلة   سورة العاديات

إِنَّ الَّذِينَ كَفَرُوا مِنْ أَهْلِ الْكِتَٰبِ وَالْمُشْرِكِينَ فِى نَارِ جَهَنَّمَ

خَٰلِدِينَ فِيهَا أُو۟لَٰٓئِكَ هُمْ شَرُّ الْبَرِيَّةِ ۝٦ إِنَّ الَّذِينَ ءَامَنُوا

وَعَمِلُوا الصَّٰلِحَٰتِ أُو۟لَٰٓئِكَ هُمْ خَيْرُ الْبَرِيَّةِ ۝٧ جَزَآؤُهُمْ

عِندَ رَبِّهِمْ جَنَّٰتُ عَدْنٍ تَجْرِى مِن تَحْتِهَا الْأَنْهَٰرُ خَٰلِدِينَ

فِيهَآ أَبَدًا رَّضِىَ اللَّهُ عَنْهُمْ وَرَضُوا عَنْهُ ذَٰلِكَ لِمَنْ خَشِىَ رَبَّهُ ۝٨

سُورَةُ الزَّلْزَلَةِ

بِسْمِ اللَّهِ الرَّحْمَٰنِ الرَّحِيمِ

إِذَا زُلْزِلَتِ الْأَرْضُ زِلْزَالَهَا ۝١ وَأَخْرَجَتِ الْأَرْضُ أَثْقَالَهَا ۝٢ وَقَالَ

الْإِنسَٰنُ مَا لَهَا ۝٣ يَوْمَئِذٍ تُحَدِّثُ أَخْبَارَهَا ۝٤ بِأَنَّ رَبَّكَ أَوْحَىٰ لَهَا ۝٥

يَوْمَئِذٍ يَصْدُرُ النَّاسُ أَشْتَاتًا لِّيُرَوْا أَعْمَٰلَهُمْ ۝٦ فَمَن يَعْمَلْ

مِثْقَالَ ذَرَّةٍ خَيْرًا يَرَهُ ۝٧ وَمَن يَعْمَلْ مِثْقَالَ ذَرَّةٍ شَرًّا يَرَهُ ۝٨

سُورَةُ العَادِيَاتِ

بِسْمِ اللَّهِ الرَّحْمَٰنِ الرَّحِيمِ

وَالْعَٰدِيَٰتِ ضَبْحًا ۝١ فَالْمُورِيَٰتِ قَدْحًا ۝٢ فَالْمُغِيرَٰتِ

صُبْحًا ۝٣ فَأَثَرْنَ بِهِ نَقْعًا ۝٤ فَوَسَطْنَ بِهِ جَمْعًا ۝٥

١٨

الجزء الثلاثون — سُورَةُ الْقَارِعَةِ — سُورَةُ التَّكَاثُرِ

إِنَّ الْإِنسَٰنَ لِرَبِّهِۦ لَكَنُودٌ ﴿٦﴾ وَإِنَّهُۥ عَلَىٰ ذَٰلِكَ لَشَهِيدٌ ﴿٧﴾ وَإِنَّهُۥ لِحُبِّ

الْخَيْرِ لَشَدِيدٌ ﴿٨﴾ ۞ أَفَلَا يَعْلَمُ إِذَا بُعْثِرَ مَا فِى الْقُبُورِ ﴿٩﴾

وَحُصِّلَ مَا فِى الصُّدُورِ ﴿١٠﴾ إِنَّ رَبَّهُم بِهِمْ يَوْمَئِذٍ لَّخَبِيرٌۢ ﴿١١﴾

سُورَةُ الْقَارِعَةِ

بِسْمِ اللَّهِ الرَّحْمَٰنِ الرَّحِيمِ

الْقَارِعَةُ ﴿١﴾ مَا الْقَارِعَةُ ﴿٢﴾ وَمَا أَدْرَىٰكَ مَا الْقَارِعَةُ ﴿٣﴾ يَوْمَ

يَكُونُ النَّاسُ كَالْفَرَاشِ الْمَبْثُوثِ ﴿٤﴾ وَتَكُونُ الْجِبَالُ كَالْعِهْنِ

الْمَنفُوشِ ﴿٥﴾ فَأَمَّا مَن ثَقُلَتْ مَوَٰزِينُهُۥ ﴿٦﴾ فَهُوَ فِى عِيشَةٍ

رَّاضِيَةٍ ﴿٧﴾ وَأَمَّا مَنْ خَفَّتْ مَوَٰزِينُهُۥ ﴿٨﴾ فَأُمُّهُۥ هَاوِيَةٌ ﴿٩﴾

وَمَا أَدْرَىٰكَ مَا هِيَهْ ﴿١٠﴾ نَارٌ حَامِيَةٌۢ ﴿١١﴾

سُورَةُ التَّكَاثُرِ

بِسْمِ اللَّهِ الرَّحْمَٰنِ الرَّحِيمِ

أَلْهَىٰكُمُ التَّكَاثُرُ ﴿١﴾ حَتَّىٰ زُرْتُمُ الْمَقَابِرَ ﴿٢﴾ كَلَّا سَوْفَ تَعْلَمُونَ ﴿٣﴾ ثُمَّ

كَلَّا سَوْفَ تَعْلَمُونَ ﴿٤﴾ كَلَّا لَوْ تَعْلَمُونَ عِلْمَ الْيَقِينِ ﴿٥﴾ لَتَرَوُنَّ الْجَحِيمَ ﴿٦﴾

ثُمَّ لَتَرَوُنَّهَا عَيْنَ الْيَقِينِ ﴿٧﴾ ثُمَّ لَتُسْـَٔلُنَّ يَوْمَئِذٍ عَنِ النَّعِيمِ ﴿٨﴾

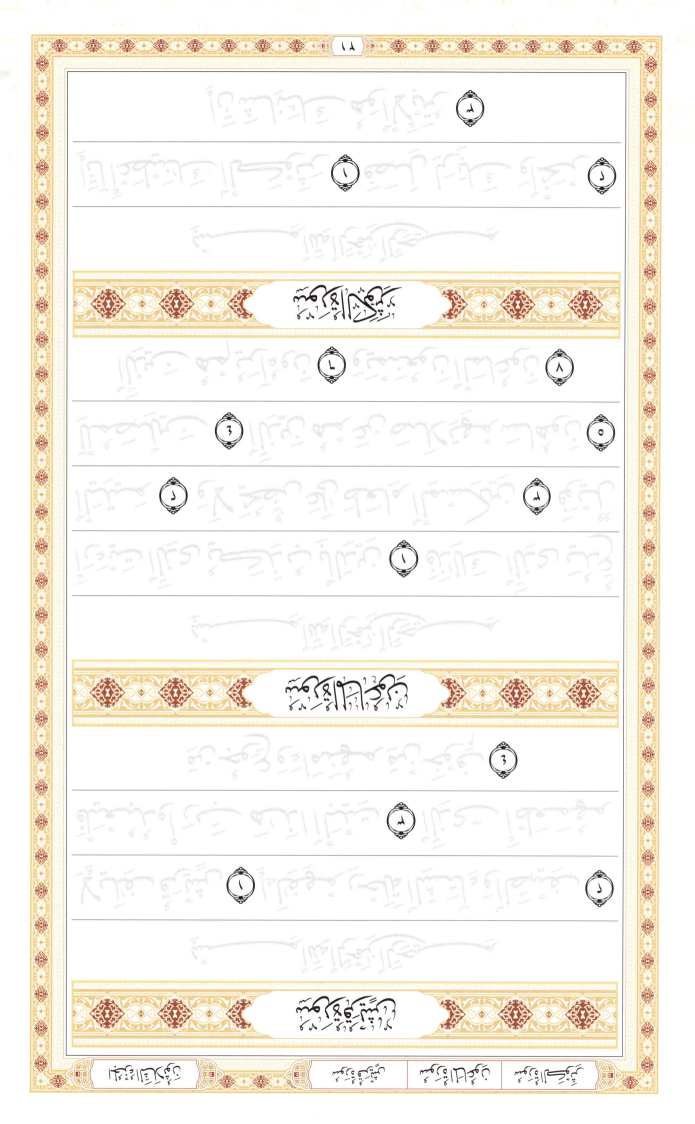

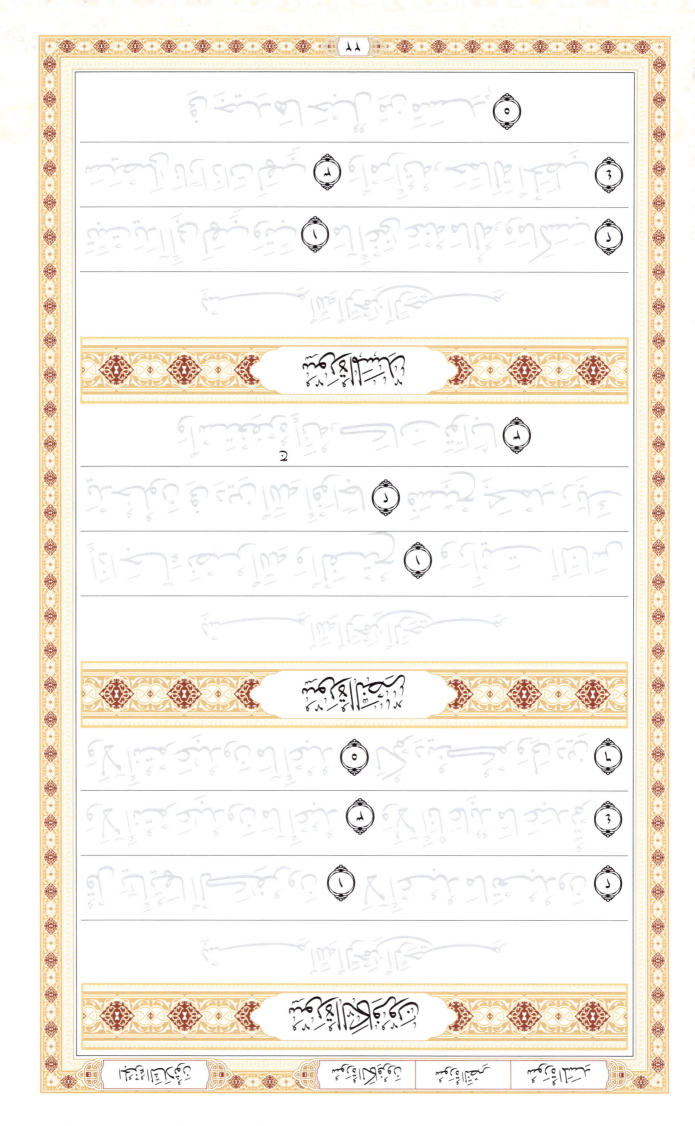

Quran Completion Du'a

اللَّهُمَّ ارْحَمْنِى بِالقُرْآنِ وَاجْعَلْهُ لِى إِمَامًا وَنُورًا وَهُدًى وَرَحْمَةً اللَّهُمَّ ذَكِّرْنِى مِنْهُ مَا نَسِيتُ وَعَلِّمْنِى مِنْهُ مَا جَهِلْتُ وَارْزُقْنِى تِلَاوَتَهُ آنَاءَ اللَّيْلِ وَأَطْرَافَ النَّهَارِ وَاجْعَلْهُ لِى حُجَّةً يَا رَبَّ العَالَمِينَ

اللَّهُمَّ إِنِّى أَسْأَلُكَ خَيْرَ المَسْأَلَةِ وَخَيْرَ الدُّعَاءِ وَخَيْرَ النَّجَاحِ وَخَيْرَ العِلْمِ وَخَيْرَ العَمَلِ وَخَيْرَ الثَّوَابِ وَخَيْرَ الحَيَاةِ وَخَيْرَ المَمَاتِ وَثَبِّتْنِى وَثَقِّلْ مَوَازِينِى وَحَقِّقْ إِيمَانِى وَارْفَعْ دَرَجَتِى وَتَقَبَّلْ صَلَاتِى وَاغْفِرْ خَطِيئَاتِى وَأَسْأَلُكَ العُلَا مِنَ الجَنَّةِ

اللَّهُمَّ إِنِّى أَسْأَلُكَ مُوجِبَاتِ رَحْمَتِكَ وَعَزَائِمِ مَغْفِرَتِكَ وَالسَّلَامَةَ مِنْ كُلِّ إِثْمٍ وَالغَنِيمَةَ مِنْ كُلِّ بِرٍّ وَالفَوْزَ بِالجَنَّةِ وَالنَّجَاةَ مِنَ النَّارِ

اللَّهُمَّ لَا تَدَعْ لَنَا ذَنْبًا إِلَّا غَفَرْتَهُ وَلَا هَمًّا إِلَّا فَرَّجْتَهُ وَلَا دَيْنًا إِلَّا قَضَيْتَهُ وَلَا حَاجَةً مِنْ حَوَائِجِ الدُّنْيَا وَالآخِرَةِ إِلَّا قَضَيْتَهَا يَاأَرْحَمَ الرَّاحِمِينَ

اللَّهُمَّ أَحْسِنْ عَاقِبَتَنَا فِى الأُمُورِ كُلِّهَا وَأَجِرْنَا مِنْ خِزْيِ الدُّنْيَا وَعَذَابِ الآخِرَةِ اللَّهُمَّ إِنِّى أَسْأَلُكَ عِيشَةً هَنِيَّةً وَمِيتَةً سَوِيَّةً وَمَرَدًّا غَيْرَ مُخْزٍ وَلَا فَاضِحٍ

اللَّهُمَّ اقْسِمْ لَنَا مِنْ خَشْيَتِكَ مَا تَحُولُ بِهِ بَيْنَنَا وَبَيْنَ مَعْصِيَتِكَ وَمِنْ طَاعَتِكَ مَا تُبَلِّغُنَا بِهَا جَنَّتَكَ وَمِنَ اليَقِينِ مَا تُهَوِّنُ بِهِ عَلَيْنَا مَصَائِبَ الدُّنْيَا وَمَتِّعْنَا بِأَسْمَاعِنَا وَأَبْصَارِنَا وَقُوَّتِنَا مَا أَحْيَيْتَنَا وَاجْعَلْهُ الوَارِثَ مِنَّا وَاجْعَلْ ثَأْرَنَا عَلَى مَنْ ظَلَمَنَا وَانْصُرْنَا عَلَى مَنْ عَادَانَا وَلَا تَجْعَلْ مُصِيبَتَنَا فِى دِينِنَا وَلَا تَجْعَلِ الدُّنْيَا أَكْبَرَ هَمِّنَا وَلَا مَبْلَغَ عِلْمِنَا وَلَا تُسَلِّطْ عَلَيْنَا مَنْ لَا يَرْحَمُنَا

رَبَّنَا آتِنَا فِى الدُّنْيَا حَسَنَةً وَفِى الآخِرَةِ حَسَنَةً وَقِنَا عَذَابَ النَّارِ وَصَلَّى اللهُ عَلَى سَيِّدِنَا وَنَبِيِّنَا مُحَمَّدٍ وَعَلَى آلِهِ وَأَصْحَابِهِ الأَخْيَارِ وَسَلَّمَ تَسْلِيمًا كَثِيرًا

Index

INFORMATION

REVEALED	AYAAT	السورة	JUZ
مكية	7	الفاتحة	الجزء الأول
مدنية	286	البقرة	الجزء الأول
مدنية	200	آل عمران	الجزء الثالث
مدنية	176	النساء	الجزء الرابع
مدنية	120	المائدة	الجزء السادس
مكية	165	الأنعام	الجزء السابع
مكية	206	الأعراف	الجزء الثامن
مدنية	75	الأنفال	الجزء التاسع
مدنية	129	التوبة	الجزء العاشر
مكية	109	يونس	الجزء الحادي عشر
مكية	123	هود	الجزء الحادي عشر
مكية	111	يوسف	الجزء الثاني عشر
مدنية	43	الرعد	الجزء الثالث عشر
مكية	52	إبراهيم	الجزء الثالث عشر
مكية	99	الحجر	الجزء الرابع عشر
مكية	128	النحل	الجزء الرابع عشر
مكية	111	الإسراء	الجزء الخامس عشر
مدنية	110	الكهف	الجزء الخامس عشر
مدنية	98	مريم	الجزء السادس عشر
مدنية	135	طه	الجزء السادس عشر
مدنية	112	الأنبياء	الجزء السابع عشر
مدنية	78	الحج	الجزء السابع عشر
مكية	118	المؤمنون	الجزء الثامن عشر
مدنية	64	النور	الجزء الثامن عشر
مدنية	77	الفرقان	الجزء الثامن عشر
مدنية	227	الشعراء	الجزء التاسع عشر
مدنية	93	النمل	الجزء التاسع عشر
مدنية	88	القصص	الجزء العشرون
مدنية	69	العنكبوت	الجزء العشرون
مدنية	60	الروم	الجزء الحادي
مدنية	34	لقمان	والعشرون
مدنية	30	السجدة	الجزء الحادي
مدنية	73	الأحزاب	والعشرون
مدنية	54	سبأ	الجزء الحادي
مدنية	45	فاطر	والعشرون
مدنية	83	يس	الجزء الحادي
مدنية	181	الصافات	والعشرون
مدنية	88	ص	الجزء الثاني والعشرون

REVEALED	AYAAT	السورة	JUZ
مدنية	75	الزمر	الجزء الثالث والعشرون
مدنية	85	غافر	الجزء الرابع والعشرون
مدنية	54	فصلت	الجزء الرابع والعشرون
مدنية	53	الشورى	الجزء الخامس والعشرون
مدنية	89	الزخرف	الجزء الخامس والعشرون
مدنية	59	الدخان	الجزء الخامس والعشرون
مدنية	37	الجاثية	الجزء الخامس والعشرون
مدنية	35	الأحقاف	الجزء الخامس والعشرون
مدنية	38	محمد	الجزء السادس والعشرون
مدنية	29	الفتح	الجزء السادس والعشرون
مدنية	18	الحجرات	الجزء السادس والعشرون
مدنية	45	ق	الجزء السادس والعشرون
مدنية	60	الذاريات	الجزء السادس والعشرون
مدنية	49	الطور	الجزء السابع والعشرون
مدنية	62	النجم	الجزء السابع والعشرون
مكية	55	القمر	الجزء السابع والعشرون
مدنية	78	الرحمن	الجزء السابع والعشرون
مدنية	96	الواقعة	الجزء السابع والعشرون
مدنية	29	الحديد	الجزء السابع والعشرون
مدنية	22	المجادلة	الجزء الثامن والعشرون
مدنية	24	الحشر	الجزء الثامن والعشرون
مدنية	13	الممتحنة	الجزء الثامن والعشرون
مدنية	14	الصف	الجزء الثامن والعشرون
مدنية	11	الجمعة	الجزء الثامن والعشرون
مدنية	11	المنافقون	الجزء الثامن والعشرون
مدنية	18	التغابن	الجزء الثامن والعشرون
مدنية	12	الطلاق	الجزء الثامن والعشرون
مدنية	12	التحريم	الجزء الثامن والعشرون
مكية	30	الملك	الجزء التاسع والعشرون
مكية	52	القلم	الجزء التاسع والعشرون
مكية	52	الحاقة	الجزء التاسع والعشرون
مكية	44	المعارج	الجزء التاسع والعشرون
مكية	28	نوح	الجزء التاسع والعشرون
مكية	28	الجن	الجزء التاسع والعشرون
مكية	20	المزّمّل	الجزء التاسع والعشرون
مكية	56	المدّثر	الجزء التاسع والعشرون
مكية	40	القيامة	الجزء التاسع والعشرون
مدنية	31	الإنسان	الجزء التاسع والعشرون

REVEALED	AYAAT	السورة	JUZ
مكية	50	المرسلات	الجزء التاسع والعشرون
مكية	40	النبأ	الجزء الثلاثون
مكية	46	النازعات	الجزء الثلاثون
مكية	42	عبس	الجزء الثلاثون
مكية	29	التكوير	الجزء الثلاثون
مكية	19	الإنفطار	الجزء الثلاثون
مكية	36	المطففين	الجزء الثلاثون
مكية	25	الانشقاق	الجزء الثلاثون
مكية	22	البروج	الجزء الثلاثون
مكية	17	الطارق	الجزء الثلاثون
مكية	19	الأعلى	الجزء الثلاثون
مكية	26	الغاشية	الجزء الثلاثون
مكية	30	الفجر	الجزء الثلاثون
مكية	20	البلد	الجزء الثلاثون
مكية	15	الشمس	الجزء الثلاثون
مكية	21	الليل	الجزء الثلاثون
مكية	11	الضحى	الجزء الثلاثون
مكية	8	الشرح	الجزء الثلاثون
مكية	8	التين	الجزء الثلاثون
مكية	19	العلق	الجزء الثلاثون
مكية	5	القدر	الجزء الثلاثون
مدنية	8	البينة	الجزء الثلاثون
مدنية	8	الزلزلة	الجزء الثلاثون
مكية	11	العاديات	الجزء الثلاثون
مكية	11	القارعة	الجزء الثلاثون
مكية	8	التكاثر	الجزء الثلاثون
مكية	3	العصر	الجزء الثلاثون
مكية	9	الهُمَزَة	الجزء الثلاثون
مكية	5	الفيل	الجزء الثلاثون
مكية	4	قريش	الجزء الثلاثون
مكية	7	الماعون	الجزء الثلاثون
مكية	3	الكوثر	الجزء الثلاثون
مكية	6	الكافرون	الجزء الثلاثون
مدنية	3	النصر	الجزء الثلاثون
مكية	5	المسد	الجزء الثلاثون
مكية	4	الإخلاص	الجزء الثلاثون
مدنية	5	الفلق	الجزء الثلاثون
مكية	6	الناس	الجزء الثلاثون